Febr. 2019

James

with love from:

Uncle Jem & Auntie Ria

Michael, Talitha, Jillian

Hendrik, Robert & Edward x

The Word of the King Series

David
and Goliath

by

Cor Van Rijswijk

Illustrated by Rino Visser

INHERITANCE PUBLICATIONS
NEERLANDIA, ALBERTA, CANADA
PELLA, IOWA, U.S.A.

National Library of Canada Cataloguing in Publication Data
Rijswijk, Cor van, 1939-
David and Goliath / by Cor Van Rijswijk ; illustrated by Rino Visser.

(The Word of the King series)
Translation of: David en Reus Goliath.
ISBN 1-894666-23-2

1. David, King of Israel—Juvenile literature. 2. Goliath (Biblical giant)—
Juvenile literature. I. Visser, Rino. II. Title. III. Series.

BS580.D3R5513 2003   j222'.4309505   C2003-910232-7

Library of Congress Cataloging-in-Publication Data
Rijswijk, Cor van, 1939-
  [David en Reus Goliath. English]
  David and Goliath / by Cor Van Rijswijk ; illustrated by Rino Visser.
    p. cm. — (The Word of the King series)
Summary: A chapter-book retelling of the Old Testament story about
David, a shepherd boy who bravely volunteered to fight the giant Goliath
knowing that God would be with him.
  ISBN 1-894666-23-2
  1. David, King of Israel—Juvenile literature. 2. Goliath (Biblical
giant)—Juvenile literature. [1. David, King of Israel. 2. Goliath
(Biblical giant) 3. Bible stories—O.T.] I. Visser, Rino, ill. II.
Title.
  BS580.D3R5513 2003
  222'.4309505—dc21
                                                              2002156698

Originally published as *David en Reus Goliath* (1995)
by Uitgeverij/Boekhandel Gebr. Koster, Barneveld, The Netherlands
Published with permission.

Translated by Roelof & Theresa Janssen
Cover Painting and Illustrations by Rino Visser

Contents

The Word of the King Series

Abraham's Sacrifice

Gideon Blows the Trumpet

David and Goliath

Audio recordings of these books
are available on Compact Disc.

Dutch titles are also available from

Inheritance Publications
Box 154, Neerlandia, Alberta Canada T0G 1R0
Tel. (780) 674 3949
Web site: http://www.telusplanet.net/public/inhpubl/webip/ip.htm
E-Mail inhpubl@telusplanet.net

1. Looking for David

Through the fields
walked a man.
He was looking around,
searching here
and searching there.
Was he looking
for someone?

From time to time
he would cry out:
"David! David!"
Then he would
look around again.
He gazed
into the distance.
"Where can
that boy be?"
he wondered aloud.

Who was the man
walking through the field?
His name was Jesse,
and he was
the father of David.
He had a job for David.
It was something
very important.

Father Jesse was
very sad and worried.
Three of his sons
were soldiers.
They were with the king
on the battlefield.
Were they still alive?
Did they have
enough to eat?
"David should go
and visit them,"
sighed Father Jesse.
But where was David?

At last he spotted him:
David was walking toward him.
Father Jesse was relieved.
"Come, David,"
he called out.
"You must do something for me."

2. The Shepherd Boy

David was a shepherd,
a very fine shepherd,
for he took very good care
of his sheep.
Whenever one
of the sheep got lost
or wandered far away,
he would look for it
until he found it.
If a wild beast
came near,
he would chase it away.
Once a lion
came out of the woods.
The lion rushed forward
and seized a lamb
from the flock.
But David saw the lion
just in time.
He killed it
with a heavy club.
Another time
he killed a bear.
Then David
thanked the Lord.

Yes, David was a shepherd
who feared the Lord.

But he was more
than a shepherd.
He was also a poet
who made up
beautiful songs
to sing to the LORD.
When it was quiet
in the fields,
he would sing
while playing his harp.
He sang about
the glory of the LORD,
and he knew
the LORD loved him.
He knew that the LORD
always took very
good care of him.

David asked someone
to watch the sheep.
Then he turned
in his father's direction.
Why was his father
calling him?
Was he supposed
to go on a journey
and visit his brothers?
Quickly David walked
toward his father.

3. Visiting His Brothers

"David, my son,
I am worried;
I am concerned
about your brothers.
I want you to go
and visit them.
Take along some
grain and bread,
and give it to them.
Take some
cheeses too.
Give them to the
commander of the army."

The next day
David woke up early
and began
his long journey.
He understood
his father's concern.
Wars were dreadful.
Many people were killed.

David knew very well
why there was a war.
The people of Israel
had stopped listening to the Lord,
and so the Lord said to His people,

"They disobeyed the LORD*'s command*
To slay the peoples of the land,
But there they mingled with the nations.
They learned how in their sins to share,
Served Canaan's vain abominations;
Its gods became for them a snare."[1]

That is why the LORD
was punishing them.
It was a terrible punishment.
Soldiers from an enemy nation
invaded the land of Israel.
They destroyed houses;
they burned the grain;
they killed some of the people.

It was not
the LORD's fault
that these
things happened.
It was the
people's own fault.
They had strayed
away from God.
David understood
how bad
things were.
And he felt
very sad about it.

---

[1] Psalm 106:17 in the rhymed version of the *Book of Praise: Anglo-Genevan Psalter.*

4. What Did He See?

David found his brothers
in the camp.
They were sitting together.
They were not talking,
and they seemed
very frightened.
Was something wrong
with them?
It was not that they were sick.
Why did they look so afraid?

In the distance they heard a sound.
It was the sound of heavy footsteps.
"There he comes again!"
said a soldier.
All the men were frightened
as they looked into the valley.

David also looked.
He saw a very tall man
coming near.
The man was a giant,
and he was strangely dressed.
He was wearing a suit
of shining bronze.
Even his legs were covered
by bronze plates.
On his head was a helmet;

it, too, was made of bronze.
His strong hand
held a large spear
with a sharp point.
And he carried
a sharp sword.

Beside him walked a man
who carried his shield.
The man looked small
next to the giant.

David looked at the giant in fear.
Now he understood
why his brothers were so silent
and so afraid.
No wonder:
Who would not tremble
at such a sight?

19

5. Goliath, the Giant

The giant spoke,
and the soldiers listened.
The giant's name
was Goliath.
He mocked Saul,
the king of Israel.
King Saul was
a brave man
and was not
easily frightened,
but now he was
full of fear
as he heard
the giant's words.
The giant mocked the king.
He also mocked his soldiers.
"Who dares to fight with me?"
he demanded.
The sound of his voice
was harsh.
His dark eyes looked angry.

"Who dares?"
he shouted again.
No one dared.
Not the king.
Not David's brothers.
Not a single soldier in Saul's army.

The giant also mocked
the people of Israel,
who were the people of God.
"Ha! Now all of you know
that I am the strongest.
No one can beat me.
You are weak,
and so is your God.
Your God cannot help you.
No one is as great
and strong as I am.
Come on, then!
Who dares to fight with me?"

No one stepped forward,
no one dared.
Then the giant began
to shout again.
He even began to curse
and swear.
David shuddered at his words,
and he felt pain in his heart.
How terrible!

The giant was scornful.
He thought he could do
whatever he wanted.
He even dared to mock the LORD!
He cursed openly at the LORD.
How terrible!

The brothers told David
that it was nothing new.
It had gone on for weeks.
Every morning
and every evening
the giant stepped
into the valley to mock.
Yet there was no one
who dared to walk up
to that giant
and do battle with him.
The giant was just too tall.
He was too strong
and too mighty!

6. I Will Fight With the Giant

"I will fight with the giant."
It was David speaking
these bold words.

David was upset
as he listened
to the giant
mocking and cursing.
He could not stand
it any longer.
It was so terrible!
The LORD is holy.
The LORD is good.
"I will kill that wicked man!"
said David.

Their countless evil deeds
Will slay the wicked in the end.
All those who hate the righteous ones
He'll to perdition send.[2]

The soldiers were amazed.
They looked up.
David's brothers got angry.
Who did David think he was?
The King also heard
what David was saying.
He called for David to come to him.

---

[2] Psalm 34:9a from the *Book of Praise*.

"What did I hear, David?
Do you want to fight with that strong man?
Do you really think you can do that?"

David answered the king.
"I cannot fight
that strong man," he explained.
"I am not strong.
I have never harmed
anyone.
But the LORD
will help me.
Once He helped
me kill a lion.
He also helped me kill a bear.
They were only wild beasts,
but Goliath mocks
and curses God!
The LORD wants me
to kill Goliath.
Certainly, my king, the LORD will help me.
Sometimes I sing:

The Angel of the LORD
Always encamps around all those
Who fear Him and exalt His Name;
God saves them from their woes.
O come, then, taste and see
That He, the LORD, is good and just.
Blest is the man who turns to Him
And puts in Him his trust."[3]

---

[3] Psalm 34:3 from the *Book of Praise*.

7. Not in a Suit of Armour

"You are very brave, my boy,"
said King Saul.
"No one dares to fight the giant.
But you are not afraid to do it!
However, I cannot let you go
to the giant
dressed like a boy.
You need armour of some kind.
You must wear
some bronze protection.
That would be
much safer for you.
Then you will look
more like a soldier,
and it will be harder
for the giant to hurt you."

The king was quick about it:
there came his servant
with a heavy coat of armour.
At once David slipped into it.
He tried his best to walk,
but he just could not.
"I am too small for this armour,"
said David.
"I am not strong enough to wear it."
Quickly he took off the armour.
"I will go to the giant

as a shepherd,
and not
as a soldier.
The LORD,
not I,
will kill that
blasphemer.
The LORD
does not want me
to wear
a suit of armour.
He wants me
to trust
in Him alone.
The LORD
will be glorified;
I must get no glory
from this battle."

The soldiers looked
at the shepherd boy.
There was respect
in their eyes.
They knew David
would not be alone:
David was going
with God!

8. A Tall Man and a Small Man

"The giant is coming again!"
The soldiers trembled.
They cried out in fear.
They heard his heavy footsteps
and the sound of his armour.
There he stood, straight and tall,
before them, in the valley.
They stared at him.
What a mighty man!

"Who dares to attack me?"
the giant cried.
"Is there no one?
Is there not
one soldier
who dares to
fight with me?"
The giant
laughed.
He was mocking
the people
of God.

But then a young lad
walked toward him.
It was David, the shepherd boy.
He had just picked up
five smooth stones from a brook

and put them in his shepherd's bag.
In one hand he held a sling,
like a leather belt.
In his other hand he held his staff.
These were the same things he used
when he tended the sheep.
With the staff
he chased away wild beasts.
With his sling
he threw pebbles
at sheep that wandered away.
When the pebbles struck the sheep,
they quickly returned to the fold.

And now David walked toward the giant,
carrying his staff and his sling.
"How does he dare?"
some soldiers whispered.

David kept walking calmly.
Soon he was down in the valley too!
There they stood:
a tall man
and
a small man.

9. The Angry Giant

When the giant saw David,
he became very angry.
Did the Israelites think
he wanted to fight
with a boy?
The boy was not even
wearing any armour!
He was not even a soldier!
Anyone could see that.

The giant was angry.
He began to shout.
Rough, angry words
tumbled from his throat.
"What are you doing here?
Do you think
you can fight with me?
All you have is a stick!
Do you think I am a dog?
Are you going
to chase me away with a stick?
I will kill you with a spear
and then the wild beasts
will eat you!
I am the strongest man
in all the world.
No one can kill me.
You are small, but I am tall."

Goliath was very,
very angry.
He did not want
to fight with a boy.
That was no challenge
for him.
He walked toward David
with great strides.
But David was not afraid;
he knew the Lord was with him.
The Lord would help him.

God shall arise and by His might
Put all His enemies to flight;
In conquest shall He quell them.[4]

---

[4] Psalm 68:1a from the *Book of Praise*.

10. David Answers the Giant

David watched
as the giant came closer and closer.
But he was not afraid.
He knew the Lord would help him;
he was sure of it.

For this I know, that God is at my side.
In Him, whose word I praise, I do confide.[5]

The Lord was with him.
Now no one could hurt him,
not even the giant.

Once he was close to the giant
David started speaking to him:
"You have come to me
with a sword and a spear;
I only have a sling and a stick.
But I will be victorious, Goliath!
You have mocked the Lord,
and you have cursed His Name.
The Lord heard you,
and now He has sent me to punish you!
I am coming to you
in the Name of the Lord.
That is why I will be the victor.

---

[5] Psalm 56:4a from the *Book of Praise*.

Today everyone will know
that there is a God in Israel.
You think you will feed my flesh
to the wild beasts.
That will not happen.
Instead the LORD will give you
and also your friends
to the birds and the wild beasts
and let them eat you.
The LORD will put you to death."

Then David spoke no more.
The time for talking was past.

The giant had had enough.
He refused to listen
to any more bold words.
Just a few more strides
and he could reach David with his sword . . .

Whatever David was going to do,
he would have to be quick about it.

11. The Young Hero

And he was quick:
he took a stone from his bag.
He put it in the sling.
The stone flew through the air . . .

"Thunk!"
The stone struck the giant.
It lodged in his head;
it drove deep into his forehead.
For a moment the giant swayed.
Then he fell flat to the ground.

David did not wait, but ran.
He ran forward
and seized the sword of Goliath.
David killed the giant
with his own sword.

From His high heavens He reached down to take me
Out of the waters — He did not forsake me!
He saved me from my fiercest enemy
And from my haters much too strong for me.[6]

It was very quiet in the valley.
King Saul and his soldiers stood amazed.
Could they believe their eyes?

---

[6] Psalm 18:6a from the *Book of Praise*.

The Philistines
were also amazed.
Surely it wasn't true!
Could that boy have
killed the giant?

12. Peace

But it was true.
Suddenly everyone saw it:
David had killed the giant.
Goliath lay on the ground
in a pool of blood.
King Saul and his soldiers
shouted for joy,
"The giant is dead!
The giant is dead!"

The enemy soldiers
also saw it.
Their tall friend
was dead.
They cried out in fear,
"Flee!
We must flee!"
And they ran
for their lives.

Soon there were
no enemies left.
All the enemy soldiers
had run away.
The people rejoiced.
The war was over!
Now there was peace
in the land of Israel.

Sing a Psalm of joy,
Shout with holy fervour.
All your skills employ;
With your heart and soul
Jacob's God extol.
He is our Preserver.[7]

"David, the shepherd boy,
is a hero,
for he has killed the giant.
The LORD has
delivered us
from a terrible enemy
by the hand of David.
To God alone
be all the glory!"
Such were the
words and songs
coming from
the people of Israel.

Thy people all will rest
By Thee so richly blest,
Since Thou with them abidest.[8]

---

[7] Psalm 81:1 from the *Book of Praise*.

[8] Psalm 3:4d from the *Book of Praise*.

13. The Great Son of David

A man was praying.
He was so full of sorrow
that tears ran down his face.

This was his prayer:

"Look upon my great affliction
And my troubles, LORD, behold;
Grant me full and free remission
Of my trespasses untold."[9]

The man knew that his heart was evil.
He knew he was at war with God.
The prince of darkness
was living in his heart.
That prince was even greater and more evil
than the giant killed by David.
There was no man
who could chase away such an enemy.
Not even David,
the heroic shepherd boy,
could chase such an enemy from his heart.
And the man himself
could not do it either!
Still, there had to be Someone
who could chase away
the enemy in the man's heart.

---

[9] Psalm 25:9a from the *Book of Praise*.

And there was Someone:
the great Son of David,
who is our Lord Jesus Christ.
He is the greatest Hero.
Only He can destroy
the prince of darkness
and make peace.

The man continued to pray:

"Hear Thou my cry, give ear to my request;
O Lord, do not my tears ignore.
For I with Thee am but a passing guest,
As all my fathers were before.
O turn away from me Thy watchful eye,
And give me joy before I die."[10]

The Lord heard that prayer.
The great Son of David
did chase the man's enemy away,
for the Holy Spirit of God
was working in the man's heart.
His tears dried up,
and his sorrow passed.
Joyfully he sang:

"The Lord, my God and Saviour,
In Him I will rejoice,
And, in His power exulting,
I will lift up my voice.

---

[10] Psalm 39:6 from the *Book of Praise*.

He makes my feet as nimble
As feet of graceful roes;
He lets me walk on mountains,
Beyond the reach of woes."[11]

Because the great Son of David
is our Hero,
all God's children can rejoice,

"I love the LORD, the fount of life and grace;
He heard my voice, my cry and supplication,
Inclined His ear, gave strength and consolation;
In life, in death, my heart will seek His face."[12]

---

[11] Hymn 10:10 from the *Book of Praise* (based on Habakkuk 3:19).

[12] Psalm 116:1 from the *Book of Praise*.

AUGUSTINE
THE FARMER'S BOY OF TAGASTE
P. DE ZEEUW, J.Gzn

2nd Printing

Augustine, The Farmer's Boy of Tagaste by P. De Zeeuw

C. MacDonald in *The Banner of Truth*: Augustine was one of the great teachers of the Christian Church, defending it against many heretics. This interesting publication should stimulate and motivate all readers to extend their knowledge of Augustine and his works. J. Sawyer in *Trowel & Sword*: . . . It is informative, accurate historically and theologically, and very readable. My daughter loved it (and I enjoyed it myself). An excellent choice for home and church libraries.

Time: A.D. 354-430	**Age: 9-99**
ISBN 0-921100-05-1	**Can.$7.95 U.S.$6.90**

2nd Printing

William of Orange-The Silent Prince by W.G. Van de Hulst

William of Orange
The Silent Prince
W.G. Van de Hulst

Byron Snapp in *The Counsel of Chalcedon*: Here is a Christian who persevered in the Christian faith when the cause seemed lost and he was being pursued by government authorities. Impoverished, he was offered great wealth to deny his principles. He refused. He remembered that true wealth is found in obeying God.

. . . Although written for children, this book can be greatly enjoyed by adults. No doubt Christians of all ages will be encouraged by the life of William of Orange. . . . This book is a great choice for families to read and discuss together.

Time: 1533-1584	**Age: 7-99**
ISBN 0-921100-15-9	**Can.$8.95 U.S.$7.90**

WHEN THE MORNING CAME

PIET PRINS

Struggle for Freedom Series 1

INHERITANCE PUBLICATIONS
NEERLANDIA, ALBERTA, CANADA

2nd Printing

When The Morning Came by Piet Prins

David Engelsma in the *Standard Bearer*: This is reading for Reformed children, young people, and (if I am any indication) their parents. It is the story of 12-year-old Martin Meulenberg and his family during the Roman Catholic persecution of the Reformed Christians in the Netherlands about the year 1600. A peddlar, secretly distributing Reformed books from village to village, drops a copy of Guido de Brès' *True Christian Confession* — a booklet forbidden by the Roman Catholic authorities. An evil neighbor sees the book and informs . . .

Time: 1568-1572	**Age: 10-99**
ISBN 0-921100-12-4	**Can.$9.95 U.S.$8.90**

Abraham's Sacrifice
by Cor Van Rijswijk

Abraham's Sacrifice

Cor Van Rijswijk
Illustrated by Rino Visser

Abraham was rich.
He had many cows and sheep,
donkeys and camels.
He also had lots of gold and silver.
The Lord had given him
all these animals and things.
This book is part of *The Word of the King Series*.
The purpose of this series is to present Bible stories in
such a fashion that young children can read them.
Read them to your four or five-year-old, and let your
six or seven-year-old use them as readers.

Time: Abraham **Age: 4-8**
ISBN 1-984666-21-6 **Can.$8.95 U.S.$7.90**

2nd Printing

Anak, the Eskimo Boy by **Piet Prins**

ANAK,
THE ESKIMO BOY

PIET PRINS

F. Pronk in *The Messenger*: Anak is an Eskimo Boy,
who, with his family, lives with the rest of their
tribe in the far north. The author describes their
day-to-day life as they hunt for seals, caribou, and
walruses. Anak is being prepared to take up his place
as an adult and we learn how he is introduced to
the tough way of life needed to survive in the harsh
northern climate. We also learn how Anak and his
father get into contact with the white man's civilization.
. . This book makes fascinating reading, teaching
about the ways of Eskimos, but also of the power of
the Gospel. Anyone over eight years old will enjoy
this book and learn from it.

Subject: Eskimos / Mission **Age: 7-99**
ISBN 0-921100-11-6 **Can.$6.95 U.S.$6.30**

2nd Printing

Jessica's First Prayer & Jessica's Mother
by **Hesba Stretton**

Liz Buist in *Reformed Perspective*: There is much
to be learned from this story. It is written primarily
for children, but this book is worthwhile reading
for adults as well . . . Highly recommended for young
and older.

The Sword and Trowel says (about *Jessica's First
Prayer*): One of the most tender, touching, and withal
gracious stories that we ever remember to have read.
A dear little book for our children. We are not ashamed
of having shed tears while reading it; in fact, should
have been ten times more ashamed if we had not.
The sweet portrait of the poor child Jessica is a
study, and old Daniel is perfect in his own way.

Subject: Fiction **Age: 9-99**
ISBN 0-921100-63-9 **Can.$8.95 U.S.$7.90**

Salt in His Blood
The Life of Michael De Ruyter
by William R. Rang

Liz Buist in *Reformed Perspective*: This book is a fictional account of the life of Michael de Ruyter, who as a schoolboy already preferred life at sea to being at school. . . This book is highly recommended as a novel way to acquiring knowledge of a segment of Dutch history, for avid young readers and adults alike.

Time: 1607-1676   **Age: 10-99**
ISBN 0-921100-59-0   **Can.$10.95 U.S.$9.90**

4th Printing

The Escape
by A. Van der Jagt
The Adventures of Three Huguenot
Children Fleeing Persecution

F. Pronk in *The Messenger*: This book . . . will hold its readers spellbound from beginning to end. The setting is late seventeenth century France. Early in the story the mother dies and the father is banished to be a galley slave for life on a war ship. Yet in spite of threats and punishment, sixteen-year-old John and his ten-year-old sister Manette, refuse to give up the faith they have been taught.

Time: 1685-1695   **Age: 12-99**
ISBN 0-921100-04-3   **Can.$11.95 U.S.$9.95**

2nd Printing

The Secret Mission
by A. Van der Jagt
A Huguenot's Dangerous Adventures
in the Land of Persecution

In the sequel to our best-seller, *The Escape,* John returns to France with a secret mission of the Dutch Government. At the same time he attempts to find his father.

Time: 1702-1712   **Age: 12-99**
ISBN 0-921100-18-3   **Can.$14.95 U.S.$10.95**

Judy's Own Pet Kitten by An Rook

Fay S. Lapka in *Christian Week*: Judy, presumably seven or eight years of age, is the youngest member of a farm family whose rural setting could be anywhere in Canada. The story of Judy, first losing her own kitten, then taming a wild stray cat with kittens, and finally rescuing the tiniest one from a flood, is well-told and compelling.

Subject: Fiction	**Age: 6-10**
ISBN 0-921100-34-5	**Can.$4.95 U.S.$4.50**

Susanneke by C. J. Van Doornik

Little Susanneke is happy! Tomorrow is Christmas. And Daddy has cleaned the church. But did he forget something? When it is her birthday Mommy always decorates the livingroom. And actually they will celebrate the Lord Jesus' birthday tomorrow. But the church isn't decorated at all. Could the big people have forgotten it? That is sad for the Lord. He loves us so much and now no one has thought about decorating the church for Him. She has to think about that for a moment. What should she do?

Subject: Fiction	**Age: 6-8**
ISBN 0-921100-61-2	**Can.$4.95 U.S.$4.50**

Sing to the LORD
The Children of Asaph
sing the Psalms of David
on the tunes of John Calvin

Noortje Van Middelkoop, Panflute
Lucy Bootsma, Violin
Daniel Bootsma, Cello
Harm Hoeve, Organ
Theresa Janssen, Conductor

Psalm 42:1, 2, & 5; Psalm 116:1, 2, 3, & 7; Psalm 124; Psalm 1 (Organ Solo); Psalm 49:1 & 2; Psalm 98; Psalm 121; Psalm 96:1, 2, & 8; Psalm 80:1, 2, & 3; Psalm 68 (Organ & Panflute); Psalm 25:1, 2, & 3; Song of Simeon (Hymn 18); Psalm 134.

For all ages!

Compact Disc	**Can.$21.99 U.S.$18.99**
Cassette	**Can.$14.99 U.S.$12.99**

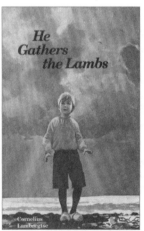